PRAISE FOR R

"Searing, commanding, and relentlessly brilliant, *Revenge Body* is a visceral journey of how to come home to yourself after a history of hurt. This collection is truly genius. Rachel Wiley makes me want to be a better writer, and there are poems in here that will welcomely haunt me for the rest of my life. What a masterpiece, what a breathtaking dive."
—MARY LAMBERT,
author of *Shame is an Ocean I Swim Across*

"Fat girls of the world will find their voice through Wiley's brilliance, and we all owe her for that."
—JES BAKER,
BLOGGER, BAKER, ADVOCATOR, *TheMilitantBaker.com*

"Wiley's poetry, first and foremost, requests that we not just tolerate, not even just respect, but celebrate difference. Wiley helps us to open ourselves up to her calls for celebration not only by giving us jokes and battle cries, but also by whispering into our ears, 'You're not perfect, are you? Me neither.'"
—VICTORIA RUSSEL,
THE DODGE

"Rachel Wiley juggles multiple topics like body shaming, visibility, depression, and identity thus making the reader feel contradictory emotions all at once. She uses humor to pinpoint how draining dating apps can be. At times it would feel like Wiley had laid herself inside out just to make her readers feel how it is to feel lonely and desperate for love, but also to have a strong desire to keep all your pieces together. The struggle is real (and sad for the most part) but Wiley makes us all privy to it, making it a little less scary."
—DEE DAS,
Book Riot

"Wiley's creative evolution is a consistent shedding of skin, with each verse, poem and collection bringing readers closer to the core of her being."

—ANDY DOWNING,
Columbus Alive

"Who we are is never a stable thing. How we see ourselves is always changing, in dynamic with the world that surrounds us. And while some become so invested in being seen as one singular thing that they waste their lives desperately hiding anything that might contradict it, Rachel Wiley's *Revenge Body* dares you to see the full spectrum of what it means to be truly and vibrantly human. Funny and profound, intimate and brash, steady-eyed and wild-hearted, Wiley explores love, family, society, heartbreak, beauty, and more, in lush, specific poems that don't flinch. We are all lucky to live in a world where a woman like Rachel Wiley trusts us enough to lift her veil, and welcome us behind the curtain."

—CRISTIN O'KEEFE APTOWICZ,
author of *How to Love the Empty Air*

"Rachel Wiley's *Revenge Body* is a blue star blooming in the throat and you *need* this heat. Wiley guides through the intimacies of family, body, love, and health with an assertive tenderness, unabashed humanity, wit and bravado. Her poems brawl with bold rhythms, bolder forms, and gut-punching confession. Through these poems, Wiley teaches us to delight in the messiness of ourselves. *Revenge Body* is a wild song of survival, sung in the face of the Miss Millies of the world."

—DIAMOND FORDE,
author of *Mother Body*

REVENGE BODY

REVENGE BODY

poems by

Rachel Wiley

Button Publishing Inc.

Minneapolis

2022

© 2022 by Rachel Wiley

◇

Published by Button Poetry / Exploding Pinecone Press

Minneapolis, MN 55403 | http://www.buttonpoetry.com

◇

All Rights Reserved
Manufactured in the United States of America
Cover design: Amy Law
ISBN 978-1-63834-000-3
26 25 24 23 22   2 3 4 5

Contents

REVENGE BODY

I.

*"Freeing yourself was one thing,
claiming ownership of that freed self was another."*

—Toni Morrison

REVENGE BODY

And
what if
the rumor is true and there
is a skinny woman imprisoned
inside my bod begging to get out
and what if I swallow my toothbrush
one morning and she were to sharpen it
against my spine and shiv her way free
leaving this fat hull behind, a cicada shell?
Will you call her a thief when she
comes
to collect everything denied her for the sake of fatness
the racks upon racks of clothes, the unsettled for love, the
unashamed sex, the glorious visibility, the basic fucking decency?
All of it handed to her in benefaction no matter how rudely she grabs.
I am not at all saying that this fat makes me any kind of saint I
am entirely capable of vengeance and pettiness in this very large
body but I am saying that I have never known this thin woman and I
cannot but imagine that she has fermented inside me, a
bitter
concentration of withholding, that she is so very hungry and so very tired of
food, that she would certainly come for what is owed her the same fat you
sneer at now the same fat sneered at without consequence might be your one
and only advantage might be a gift; might be the only barrier between you and
a pin-less grenade who would wear your wedding dress better than you ever
could while politely fucking your betrothed standing up on the very altar
where you were meant to say your vows leaving you
alone
with only
the cake for comfort

ODE TO THE INVISIBLE GIRL

guitar picks
match sticks
sage bundle lungs
pocket mirror
calloused finger-
tips
      drip
           1 drop
               invisible girl

     if you ask me, I will tell you, but you won't think to ask.
I pass.
I pass smooth like water
like blood
one swollen drop
after
another.

Mulatto comes from the Latin word for mule
Okay, so I'll be a mule,
        just not yours.
           I'll run these drops
                this culture
                a razor blade at the roof of my
                mouth
             this righteous anger
                  matchsticks in my hair
           this undeserved forgiveness
               sage smoke in my chest.

You won't think to ask,
but if you did, I would tell you:
I am the granddaughter of a great jazz & blues man
who spent his whole life with his hand wrapped around the neck
of a strung-up branch
rather than the other way around,
                    and that right there is survival.

WANT NOT

The house I grew up in, the house my parents still live in, is a
sandcastle. My mother moves from chaotic room to disordered room
accusing everyone of stealing
the eyeglasses that sit atop her head, a bifocaled crown of denial, her
faithful dogs trailing her heels, both entirely deaf, the secret to their
unwavering loyalty.

My stepfather is a retired librarian with his own stacks in the attic,
a sweet-tempered hermit crab living among towers of wobbling toys
still safe in their original packaging and comic books swaddled in
plastic. He is ordered disorder; He is not comfortable, but he is
rarely one to complain except to say, to no one in particular, that he
cannot seem to get warm.

There are eight feral cats living in what used to be my bedroom.
They hiss in unison if you don't knock before you come in, having
no doubt gotten into a shoebox of my teenage angst forgotten in the
back of the closet.

In place of family photos, the walls host ornate portraits of my
estranged brother's fists cradled in the plaster. The knuckles follow
me around the room though he hasn't laid a finger here in 20 years.

Nothing in our house is ever thrown away; it barely escapes or is
buried alive. There are floorboards still clutching strands of my
hair, wallpaper with my blood worked into the floral pattern,
veteran door hinges twisted and loose from their failed attempts
to keep me safe.

Technically, it's a 1912 American Foursquare brick house but really,
it's a sandcastle of dust and pet hair packed tight with trauma.
There are nights I dream of going
home again
as a wave.

ALL THE PILLS I TRIED BEFORE

Lexapro:
little boats on a mechanical waterfall,
a contented plummet followed by a souvenir photo;
in it I am screaming in delight,
I think.

Adderall:
without a doubt a fire sign,
insists not to be into games or drama.
Anyone who makes this claim in their dating profile
is bringing games and drama.

Wellbutrin:
smooth as a rattlesnake swallowed backward,
whole and alive, chemical grains shaking a warning all the way down
my throat. I grew venomous, grew scales, & wanted
to skin myself to make boots.

Effexor:
pretty petals plucked from poppies the color of a gentle blush,
we slept and slept and slept
without dreaming of anything at all.
Apathy is the new love.

Vyvanse:
a luxury car with cut brake lines
a smooth ride
every stop head-on
into a tree

HANDSOME, OR IN WHICH NEITHER OF US IS *THE MAN*

At the store where we have stopped
to buy the candy we will sneak
into the movies on date night, the cashier greets us with a smile,
compliments my dress, says *I look so pretty tonight*
before wondering out loud why my date isn't also dressed up,
as though she isn't standing right next to me,
paying for the candy,
doesn't she want to be pretty, too?
I cannot stop the giggle that erupts from my startled throat
at witnessing what could only be this grown woman's first ever
sighting of a real live butch
in the wild.

My date doesn't want to be pretty,
she doesn't need to want to be pretty
to be a woman. She is a woman because she tells me so.
She is a woman because there is no wrong way
to woman. She is
a woman on her terms, a woman with the lump of a soft leather
billfold in her back pocket, who holds my doors and doesn't mind that
my grandma calls her a little gentleman, wears a pair of boxer briefs
better than most men, and is the only person I've ever called daddy.
A woman who is often tipped less than the flirty femmes on the wait
staff she manages because her *not pretty* makes people uncomfortable.
My date was dressed up for date night, wearing a dress shirt,
a slightly loose necktie, pants that I'm almost certain she ironed.
When she picked me up from my house, I swooned at the cuffs of her
shirt rolled to her elbows / her tattoos peeking out / a hint of things
under the dress shirt I would trace my fingers along later.
In a similar such moment of fingers sliding along skin, I called her
beautiful. She buried her face into my neck and politely refused it,

said it wasn't her word and still she remains a woman,
a woman who grins and blushes an entire sunset when I shyly tell her
she is handsome—
the most handsome sunset I've ever seen.

NEW MOON, WHO THIS?

Tonight, the moon is a knife trick set on debridement,
hand over everything she asks for
even and especially everything that will hurt to release
What is yours will return to you with the tangles removed
and won't that be lovely?
What doesn't return was only ever visiting.

POEM FOR SUSAN "BOOMER" JENKINS

From the Australian TV Show Wentworth

And like a punch to the side of the head, there she is on my television,
everything I have worked my whole fat life to never be, embodied.
Susan "Boomer" Jenkins is a goon,
fat and loud, a graceless simple villain, unkempt and unbothered
by the revulsion no one even tries to smuggle past her.
In fact, Susan "Boomer" Jenkins shakes people down for their
revulsion and uses it to brew the finest prison grog.
Susan "Boomer" Jenkins is all fight no flight,
has never been weightless enough for flight,
only dense enough for brute force,
for destruction and she leans into this,
doesn't really know how not to.

What unsettles me most about her is the obscene way that she wants,
open mouthed and unreasonable, spilling onto everything.
If I have wasted my life attempting to cinch anything in more than
my body, it has been my wanting
for fear of it looking like a delusional appetite on a body already
appointed the mascot of greed.

Susan "Boomer" Jenkins cries publicly, cries ugly, blotchy-faced
angry, wails for her wants, tantrums for someone to stay, to fight
for her, to run into her wanting
with their own wanting,
for her to be unquestionably the source of a want as hungry
as her own, for someone to see the softness her bulk is capable of,
to root out the sweetness in her cloying.
In this way, Susan "Boomer" Jenkins is my own sloppy heart,
a greasy haired beast caged
and longing for something to float gently down in her favor
just once,
something she will not have to drag
struggling to her chest and subdue.

EXECUTIVE FUNCTIONING

I can assure you it isn't that I don't care; my truffle
pig brain broke her tether
again
and wandered off to unearth some
sweetly moldering dopamine. It's just what she knows best
and she really likes to do what she knows best.
I will eventually follow through on everything
I said I'd do after
I reheat the tea that went cold
without ever leaving the microwave. I could
take this whole world by storm if I could
keep it from wandering off
mud-stuck scrolling instagram
again
I would have returned your email sooner
except it seemed so exhausting
not that you're exhausting
but everything kind of is,
and the tea has gone cold in the microwave
again
I have half read almost every book I own
I promise I'll tell you what I thought of that one you recommended
if we are still on speaking terms by then
we might not be
It's not exactly that I forget you
like the tea reheating again in the microwave
I would never
I am trying to tell you there is a wall of radios in my head,
nearly all of them playing something I might want to hear
and every now and again something like a miracle happens
and they all play the same perfect song at the same time
and how can I not submerge then?
How can I not mourn when the silver synchronized fish cloud
remembers itself and scatters?

I will let you in on a secret.
I am most reliable on laundry day.
Everything folded and put in place the same
day it is washed. My attention can be paid
in rolled quarters and the scent of dryer sheets. It is
the one task I consistently see through
to completion even while the tea goes
cold behind the microwave door
again.
Sometimes, when it looks like I am doing absolutely nothing, I am
trying so hard to do everything
that I might not see you standing there.

GHOST ME, I'LL WRITE YOUR EULOGY

I think the great rapper Cardi B said it best when she said, "If you got a problem with me, say it now / Cause I don't wanna hear no sneak dissin' / Specially not from one you weak bitches."

Today we gather to lay to rest a double-mouthed face, one who came from a land of salt and ice, a person I called dearest, and at times best friend, same one I fed and rooted for and trusted, who I welcomed into my home, even threw them a party, carpeted the floor in balloons, filled nearly to bursting with air from my own lungs. Same one I made space for at every table I was invited to and halved my meal with, who kept fires lit in the rain with me, who I shared holidays and heartaches with not knowing, not once suspecting, that all along they were incubating a virus of resentment.

Invisible friend.

I did not see that they:
thrived best when my heart was foreclosed,
liked me best at my most shattered,
danced best to the clatter
of my brokenness. How thoughtless
knit my bones and deprive them of their music.

They slipped from my world on their own stilled tongue after they reached for some shine that was not theirs, got burnt, and chose to blame the shine rather than their own entitled hands.

They are survived by their own relentless mediocrity and some mountains that never claimed them anyway.

Today we say a final goodbye to a false bottom friend who was swallowed whole by a green and bitter moss. Their body will be interred to a planter's field among

promise-breakers, liars, back-climbers, cowards,
and the other rotting disloyal.
Perhaps not literally dead but very much gone, very much below me.
Hurt to hurt. Acid to acid. Trust to dust.

THIRTY-SIX

It is my Marilyn year
and my sex drive is laying limp on the bed
a side effect of so many pills,
the ones meant to keep me great and going,
the body going cold with the phone clutched in hand
while the one I love slips out the window
to build a proper home with someone else,
someone who would not require warming up.

THEORY OF THE ORIGIN OF WHITENESS

Whiteness was born silent
a gas leak
fed on sea water
grew quickly into a hueless swarm
took its first steps coming ashore in a world new to it
greed came in like teething
then gnashing
Whiteness marveled at its hands and their grab
everything: *mine*
it threw tantrums that wiped out whole villages of Native
when Whiteness did not have enough
hands to grab all that it wanted
it stole hands from Blackness
refused to give them back
said, *God's will*
Whiteness claims unseeable and so is God
Whiteness plays God
Whiteness doesn't play well with Others
Whiteness pouts when told to share
it is always Whiteness' turn
especially when it is definitely not Whiteness' turn
Whiteness says, *forget the past*
says, *there is no such thing as ghosts*
Whiteness haunts everything
everything
everything
everything.

When whiteness sleeps, it does so with all the lights on
and every door locked behind it.

BUG

my mother used to call me *bug*
I was born so small
surprise daughter infestation
two is a family

I was born so small
a defenseless thing in her care
two is a family
three is a crowd

a defenseless thing in her care
her son was here first
three is a crowd
mothers and sons have a special bond

her son was here first
he had magnifying glass hands
mothers and sons have a special bond
I never had a chance

he had magnifying glass hands
surprise daughter infestation
I never had a chance
my mother used to call me *bug*

WHAT WE WERE

My brother and I were children once.
Joyfully
briefly
boundless architects of blanket forts, fighter pilots of front porch
runways, raised defiant and staring down the sky. One time we flew,
feet-off-the-ground flew, and no one could tell us otherwise.
We were homemade and hand-me-down, we double dog dare ya, we
were not afraid of the dark, we ain't afraid of no ghosts, we heroes in
half shells, we home alone one and two, we drained entire two liters
of Dr Thunder and belched T.G.I.F, we had no bedtime, we had cable
television and Little Caesar's pizza pizza, we were once the greatest
cover band of a single song we played over and over again.
We were water gun assassins, wrapping paper roll jousters, sleeping
bag bobsledding Olympians of the staircase, we water fight turned
real fight, we didn't know our own strength, we made peace with
Band-Aids and ice packs and pinky promise pacts before mom
got home.

My brother grew up to be a magician.
My brother grew up to be twice as angry as he was tall
and he got so tall.
Spring-loaded goldfinches always up his sleeves
and I, his assistant
cut down with a flourish,
phantom sibling,
a dull ache at the severing point.
The days I forget I have a brother
are the same days I forget I was a child at all.

RED HERRING

For months I held it still in my mouth, a word made of glass,
$$my\ ex,$$
positive it would ribbon my tongue with its jagged wrongness.
When I finally force it past my lips, it left a dull metallic taste,
unpleasant and ultimately harmless,
less harmful at least than you saying you'd never loved me anyway.
The untruth of which sliced the soft pink of your mouth,
filled it with blood.
Your tongue flopped onto the empty sofa cushion between us,
a gasping fish.

THE WAY BACK

By the time my ex crawls from the wreckage and grasps the enormity
of her error she will also have to be aware that she can never speak
enough words, not even knotted end-to-end, to lasso me back.

If there is to be any hope at all, there will need to be a gesture
and it will need to be, at minimum, grand,
not because I no longer love her but because somehow I still do,
and her undue luck merits a proper tribute,
beginning by manifesting an instantaneous crop of fat-headed
dahlia blooms bursting firework and floral through the rough dirt
and brick shards in the empty lot across the alley from my apartment.

I expect all of the rattling bass her Chevy Impala can scrape together
to fill the air with our song so thickly that the neighbors
will be pulling lyrics from their gutters with handfuls
of soggy autumn leaves. For the grand finale,
a magic show where she pulls the lies
from her mouth like rotten teeth before baptizing
new honest gums with every salty tear I shed in her wake.

FEMME FATALE

His
first
mistake
is assuming
anything I do
is done for male
consumption, for *his*
consumption. I put my
face on artfully every mo
-rning. My time in front of
the mirror getting it just right
might appear a shallow act. He
might assume that I am the one dis
-tracted and he is not. He might assume
my walk-in closet is a temple of vanity and
not a war room when it is both. My eyeliner
stays winged so sharp it could kill a man. If I al
-low him near enough to embrace me it is only to fu
-rther sharpen my blade against the rough of his cheek.
He might assume that I am soft, that I am unarmed. I am
soft, lushly so, but I am also always armed, and I am patien
-tly waiting for that inevitable moment he makes himself com
-fortable atop my soft, drunk on his own toxicity, before I bleed him out.

SAFETY SPELL FOR SEA MONSTERS
For Leo

breathe deep and lay your weary bones on our altar
watery safehouse under the ocean
we pull the waves above our heads
a blanket fort against land dwellers who call us monsters
water might be the only thing that could ever hold us gentle
my arms and your arms are also water

we banish anyone who scavenges for blood in our water
who comes to steal golden peace from our altar
who decries the water's righteous crash without ever praising its gentle we
banish those who fear us the way they fear the endlessness of the ocean
though still fill their pockets with its gifts—those who make us monsters
and then set a bounty for our shipwrecked heads
wave away the foraging fish that nibble our heavy heads

we are still living and as necessary to living as water
we must be massive because inside we hold hearts sized for monsters and
when the tides slow into quiet hymns our chests are the most sacred altar
we are not *too much* but *so much* like our ocean
may we float deservedly gentle

the tide is a kind nurse with a bedside manner so gentle
there is nowhere better to heal our bruised knuckles our churning heads
than the salted infirmary of our ocean
there's nothing that can't be fixed in the water
nothing that can't be laid safely down in this altar
here we can expose our soft bellies though we be monsters

there is enough wrenching loneliness in being monsters
in having to convince the landlocked that we are even capable of gentle-ness, that
each scale on our bodies is a saint-stamped medal—as much altar
to softness and survival as monster—we keep the water above our heads
never our heads above the water
the ocean belongs in/to/with us—we belong in/to/with the ocean

when the blood scavengers move to run us from our rightful ocean when
they leave no choice but to show the extent to which we be monsters
to demonstrate our talent for shaking any comfort they found in our water
until every cell they possess surrenders any memory of gentle things and
they must defeatedly bow their heads
and leave in tithing their hubris on our altar

pack your lungs with all the air they hold and steal away to our ocean altar
to pray, to give thanks, to let the light and water
braid crowns around our royal heads
and rest where shipwrecks soften and at last get to be gentle

II.

"There is a sense of being in anger. A reality and presence. An awareness of worth. It is a lovely surging."

—Toni Morrison

WHAT BRINGS ME IN TODAY

My friend reaches across two time zones
every night to tell me how he might end his life,
challenges me to give him reasons to live.
No matter what time he calls, I pick up
and charm a belt from around his neck
slow-dance his sneakers back from a ledge,
or summon just enough light
in my voice to scatter pills back into their bottles.
            One day my phone goes silent,
                deathly so.
            I call him; it's one ring
            and a full voicemail box.
I smoke a scrounged bowl of sticky resin,
sleep fitfully,
dream that my teeth are tiny sandcastles
dissolving under the tide of my tongue,
dream of swallowing myself whole,
dream that I find my friend in the ocean
and we swim down together,
Homegoing King and Queen of Atlantis.
Waking up is a fish-gasping betrayal.

I call in sick to my cubicle job,
call the number on my insurance card,
ask if a therapist is covered under my plan,
call three of the referrals and leave messages.
I take the bus to a salon where
I ask to have my dead ends clipped
and my fingernails buffed and painted.
I choose a delicate pink called Rosey Future.

            I search for my friend on Google,
          tacking *obituary* on as a new surname,
            text him little red heart emojis,

look up plane tickets across two time zones,
find no wings in my bank balance,
and buy an opulent pair of discount sunglasses
to wear on the bus ride back home.

In my dirty apartment
I inventory all the pills I have,
text more lonely red heart emojis,
and think about Atlantis.

I return to work the next day
where I am reprimanded
for not having an excuse
from a doctor.
I spend my lunch break calling therapists
and gnawing my fresh manicure down to the quick.

The 9th or 10th therapist answers
after only three rings.
I take the first appointment available and after work
wear my new sunglasses
on the #2 bus for an hour
in the opposite direction from my dirty apartment.
In a sage green waiting room fogged in white noise
I fill out a clipboard of paperwork
before telling a small, kind-looking woman about my friend
who doesn't want to live anymore.

EXCUSES

Rachel is unable to come to work today for one or more
of the following reasons:

Unable to stop crying and/or shitting and/or
bleeding and/or feeling.

Car trouble.
The trouble being that she is 38 years
old and neither owns a car
or knows how to drive.

She is entirely too cool for this shit.

A water main broke and filled her apartment
like an aquarium. If she opens the door now, all the water
will get out and she will never truly know
what it's like to be a goldfish.

Someone has died
and no one noticed. She is calling off in solidarity,
in mourning, in hopes that someone might use some
of their precious sick time to mourn her one day,
too.

She woke up made entirely of fog.

She stayed up all night thinking of everything
she's ever done wrong, and she is exhausted.

She spent last night being visited by a trio of lost
ghosts who kept calling her Ebenezer.

A flock of words flew in through her window
and begged her to bake them into a poem before they
spoiled in the sky

There was a break-in and the thief made off with
her bones, leaving her to construct new ones
out of things within reach. Have you ever had to reframe
your entire body from spoons and spent toilet paper rolls?
It takes a while. She might be able to
make it in for a half day. Maybe.

DREADFUL SORRY, CLEMENTINE

September showed up on time
but summer refused to give up its seat.

The first Saturday morning without you
in 12 years, a sweating man brought me

a wooden box of ashes bearing your name etched in gold.
The cicadas started to creep into the house between the gaps
of the window screens without you here to hunt them, kill them,
leave their headless bodies at the top of the stairs for me in offering.

For your homegoing, I trapped and trained a choir of the otherworldly
insects to sing Queen's *Fat Bottom Girls*
in tribute to your well-fed memory.

and then gathered up all the neighborhood squirrels who lost
the tops of their tails to your teeth and got them to march across
the roof, a procession of furry flags flying at half-mast.

I put on my nicest black dress and rolled on the carpet still covered
in your loose fur. I could not bring myself to give it up
to the vacuum's greedy mouth.

The longest you ever let me hold you in all our time together
was that final day in the vet's office. I begged your gold sedated eyes
to forgive that I could not stay to witness you down to the last
heartbeat.
They told me a wretched dampness had gathered in your lungs,
an underhanded flash flood that swept you away right under my nose.

I'm so sorry I did not see it coming.
I would have fought it back with my own
fists and all my magic if I had.

DEEP CONDITIONING

I.

Against my mother's wishes
I shave my legs for the first time in secret when I am 10,
press down too hard, a thin ribbon of skin blooms
from the head of the razor, the first of many
bloody receipts for what I understand to be femininity.

II.

I did and do have a lot of hair, though it is thin/fine, like my
mother's, my older brother having previously absconded with
any and all DNA for the lush curls usually associated with mixed
children, perhaps the first instance of his lack of regard for any
child born after him.

III.

In 7th grade math class, Tiffany looks at me hard from across
the table before asking loud enough for everyone to hear
why my eyebrows almost touch.

IV.

I am locked in the bathroom with my clock radio/cassette player
combo blasting the same cassingle over and over, daydreaming
about Taylor Hanson and shaving between my eyebrows when
my brother pounds on the door and startles half of my left
eyebrow into the blades of the razor.

V.

My mother laughs when telling the story of my birth, of when the
nurse placed me in her arms, and she asked where the baby was
and why they handed her this tiny monkey.

VI.

My hair is thin/fine like my mother's,
it is naturally dark,
not at all like my mother's,
whom you cannot tell does not shave her legs unless
you get very close.
I cannot tell my mother does not shave her legs.

VII.

Everyone in 4th period study hall started calling Dawn
the wildebeest today because she is fat and her arms are covered in
dark hair. She cries and says she's just Italian. That night in the bath
I begin a lifelong ritual of shaving my arms from wrist to shoulder
because my great grandfather on my mom's side is also Italian and
also my arm hair is dark and also I am fatter than Dawn and I don't
need those problems.

GLOW

I am 15 and my mother has caught me fresh off the phone
in a moment of unguarded joy.
She sweeps in and cups my laughter in her hands.
It flutters wildly against her caged fingers,
she marvels loudly at the rarity of the thing,
     as though it is rare because I am selfish with my
                glow,
    as though she never saw the bloody smears of my smile
         lighting up her son's knuckles.

The trapped, delicate thing flickers out in her hands.

PROZAC 30MG

When
the doctor
asked if I was suicidal
I told her that I'd called off
work one day last week to sit on
my balcony and witness the old Victorian home
across the alley being dismantled by a crane. For years
I watched this house pass from one new owner to the next,
each excited by her potential, each sure they would be the one to fix
her, each eventually deciding she was too much work. I tell my doctor that
I feel like a house, unwieldy and unclaimed. I worry my bones might be
made of crumbling red brick. I am prescribed 3 green oils to be taken
with breakfast. They are supposed to make me feel less heavy, more gr-
ounded and mostly they work. In the event I forget to take them altog-
ether I am less person, more flock of hummingbirds hovering in a vague
person configuration tying not to get caught. Now, there are still days
even when I remember to take them, that I grow to be 50 ft tall with-
out much warning and make a mess of everything. My giant hands fum-
ble to fix the things I have broken but only make them worse. And what
I want more than anything when I am 50 ft tall is to be met with tende-
rness until I can get back to a manageable height but there are no arms
big enough to hold me when I am 50 ft tall. I am embarrassed by the sc-
ale of my neediness and just want to hide but there is nowhere to hide
when I am 50 feet tall. The medical miracle of the 3 green pills is that
even on those days when I am 50 feet tall I know now more often than I
don't know that I am a soft human woman deserving of the care and
the work to keep me standing and not a hollowed out Victorian home
anyone can pull down brick by brick.

WHEN THE FAT GIRL STAYS FAT

Her mouth says that she simply can't have any
French fries, but her thin arm slithers across the table
for the third time to pull a few from my plate.
She says I made them look *too good*. She could not resist.
She will lick the warm salt from her delicate fingers,
it will be something like seductive.
She can have everything she wants without
looking like a beast, without looking like me.

Once, I dared to enjoy an apple at a bus stop,
a large beautiful Honeycrisp apple, perfectly chilled,
and a car veered across two entire lanes of traffic to splash
my fat body with shame for being seen eating
anything at all.

When the skinny girl ran away from the dinner table to
chase the glinting edges of her collarbones, she was
sweetly coaxed back to the table with dollops of full fat
ice cream spooned into her mouth as an offering. Hail the
return of the prodigal prom queen to a gown that never
came in plus size to begin with.

Sometimes I still catch myself refusing to eat,
instead curling myself around my violently rumbling
stomach, a train I might get to ride into lightness if I can
stay onboard long enough. Hunger never made me his girl
no matter how sweetly I begged him to stay. Hunger loves
me the same as so many men, full of shame, pants still half
on for a secret heaving mistress.

When the skinny girl pleats and pins
my deflated skin to fit around her small frame,
all the still wet spit from angry mouths from when I wore it

ripen into a diamond sparkle that hangs off her hips.
People will call it something like courageous.
She is a Cinderella story;

I, the fat gourd she arrives in.
I suppose it isn't her fault.
        I do make it look too good
                —how could she possibly resist?

INTERSECTIONAL FEMINISM (AKA ACTUAL FUCKING FEMINISM) PLAYS THE DOZENS WITH WHITE FEMINISM

White Feminism is as feminist as Dr Pepper is a medical doctor,
        as Rachel Dolezal is Black,
                as an orgasm with Donald Trump would ever be real.
White Feminism so white she colonizes everything
she likes as her *spirit animal*.
This bitch has whole chunks of sacred land stuck between her teeth
but gets defensive when you let her know rather than thanking you
and cleaning out her teeth.

White Feminism's autocorrect changes appropriation to appreciation
because she uses them interchangeably.

White Feminism so white she won't see why anyone would be
    offended by her pink pussy hat,
                so white she thinks Amy Schumer is hilarious.
In fact, all of White Feminism's favorite jokes use black women
as punchlines and she doesn't understand why you refuse to laugh,
why you refuse to just
              lighten up.
White Feminism has herself one black friend (Stacey Dash),
still shows up to your Halloween party in black face tho,
thinks Beyoncé is overrated and Taylor Swift is a feminist icon tho,
thinks twerking is a sexual revolution on Miley but wants to know
why Nicki just won't respect herself tho.
White Feminism, what's good?

White Feminism acts brand new.
White Feminism isn't brand new.
White Feminism aka Women's Suffrage got some cosmetic work
done, had her blatant racism capped with complicit racism, the kind

of racism that allows her to wear a war bonnet to Coachella and call it being a free spirit. She still only marches when she benefits, still only votes in her own best interest.

White Feminism doesn't appreciate being called WHITE Feminism, doesn't understand why everything's *always got to be about race*, doesn't *see color*, and thinks *your obsession with race is frankly divisive*. Besides, Meryl Streep said, *We're all descendants of Africa!* And anyway, White Feminism smiles and swears she will unlock the door to equality and let us all in if we just hoist her through this window on our backs, and ain't that just like White Feminism, always getting up on someone else's back?

WHITE FEMINISM WATCHES
THE COLOR PURPLE

Mrs. Millie has always been kind to you people
Mrs. Millie said *your children are so clean*
It was a compliment
Say thank you to Mrs. Millie
Mrs. Millie said *your children are so clean*
Mrs. Millie forgave you your wild ways
Say thank you to Mrs. Millie
You really made it harder than it had to be
Mrs. Millie forgave you your wild ways
Did you hear that? Mrs. Millie is taking you to see your family
You made it Blacker than it had to be
Don't you know who she is?
Mrs. Millie has taken you to see your family
Mrs. Millie cannot get out of reverse
Don't you know who she is?
Those men were trying to attack Mrs. Millie
Mrs. Millie cannot get out of reverse
How could you leave her alone with them?
Those men were trying to attack Mrs. Mille
Mrs. Millie doesn't know your sister
How could you leave her alone with them?
After all she has done for you
Mrs. Millie doesn't know your sister
Be grateful, gal
After all we have done for you
It was a compliment
Be grateful, gal
Say thank you to Mrs. Millie

TO THE GIRL IN BLACKFACE ON HALLOWEEN 2012

Sometimes when I talk now it sounds a lot like screaming.
Sometimes, without meaning to, I shake roof tiles loose and rattle
windowpanes. Sometimes I wake folks out of a dead sleep.

Sometimes it gets so lonely late at night, and I know that somewhere
you are sleeping so sound even the mournful howling of the dead
can't wake you. Did you know you managed to turn me both
ear-splitting and invisible that night?

How did you know that I'd wanted
to be a thunderclap someday?

ON SIGHT

For Dez

The universe has seen fit to open its filthy mouth
and speak an abundance of woes into existence for my best girl.

I, being a fire-tempered witch,
intend now to punch this salty universe

squarely in its disrespectful mouth
and claim its jagged teeth as trophies for my mantel,

pawn its gold crowns to buy my bestest a whole heap of high-end
stability and an endless supply of the top-shelf sleep she is owed.

THE MOTHER RIDDLE

With all the suddenness of finding a rogue shard
of a broken glass with the tender bottom of your foot,
it occurs to you that you haven't talked to your mother in months.
Try as you might, you can only drum up a thimble of guilt
about not noticing sooner.

You reach out with a simple hello, half-hearted attempt
as it is, there is still a heart, obligatorily beating.
Three weeks go by with no response.
She is preparing the ground for you.
She means for you to grovel.
You know better than to hope she will concede
to not reaching out either.

This is your fault the way everything is / has always been / will
always be your fault. Your fault for staying and speaking
where her beloved son refused.
You know she would forget the name she gave you if he were to text
her with half a heart.

You decide to call this time.

Before you can dial, a graceful sphynx pads in
and stands guard at your throat.

A massive and regal feline with the face of every TV mom
you wished for and a hint of your therapist's encouraging smile.
She says you must answer three riddles
before you try to reach out to the woman whose body bore you:

    I.   If your mother disowns her own mother,
           and her mother disowns her mother before that,
           and you then disown your mother, is it a grudge
           or a genetic trait?

II. If your mother hears you being brutalized by her rageful son in another room of the house and turns the volume on the television up in response, is she still actually allowed to say she is your mother?

III. If after 15 years and lots of therapy you ask your mother to acknowledge the way she failed to protect you, and she still responds by turning the volume on the television up, and only then do you begin tugging your roots free of her, are you holding a grudge, or is the grudge holding you, like your mother should have?

PIEROGI

At a bar in Cleveland, Ohio, I am encouraged to order pierogi
for the first time, and they are brought to me still cold in the center.
While the table is aghast at the kitchen's massive Midwest faux pas,
I cannot help the wry smile that creeps across my lips for these sad
lumps of mashed potato wrapped in pastry trying so hard to be
appetizing, I nearly confuse them for my own heart.

III.

"Anger is a very intense but tiny emotion, you know. It doesn't last."

—Toni Morrison

THEORY OF THE ORIGIN OF HEAVEN

The ocean has always been.
It's the land that was coughed into existence
and slowly populated by guppies exiled to the dirt for their various
underwater criminalities. These fish died sun bleached and gasping
until eventually they didn't, until luck flopped them into cool mud
and slowly something like living
took place,
until they sprouted small legs and their scales gave way to smooth
skin. Still though they directed their pleas for
forgiveness at the blue sky in confusion.

UNBOW YOUR HEAD, SISTER

For The Pink Door Coven

My Sister adjusts my crown and I shine My Sister's crown with a sleeve. We link pinkies & flirt stars down from the sky to breathe life back into them with mouthfuls of fire-tongued kisses.

I bring food to My Sister, still hot, urge My Sister to eat, even spoon it into My Sister's mouth when needed, remind My Sister to replace the water given freely away to others, remind

My Sister the body needs its simple comforts to continue housing the strong magic of being My Sister. I become an evangelical of deserving when My Sister cannot muster the proper

righteousness. I turn My Sister's trembling hands palms up and empty into them everything my pockets hold until the weight of what I can give steadies them.

My Sister calls me by my name when everyone else forgets it, sees me even when my own mother won't. My Sister picks me up from the side of the road because My Sister would never

pass me by. My Sister blots out the shame that tailcoats my weakness, lays a hand to my bruises to remind the skin of its strength, that it did not break though it had every right to, considering

the ungentleness it was met with. My sister reminds me that the bruise will fade, that I will not. When My Sister's skin breaks, because this time it couldn't not break, I lay a hand to the split,

remind it of its incredible knitting. I whisper parables to the skin where it returns stronger and shinier – a brand-new jewel of flesh set into sturdy veteran flesh.

My Sister does not come to hush my sobs or to wipe clean my devastation. Instead, My Sister points my mourning face to the night sky. My Sister releases wails that sister my own.

My Sister & I feed our sorrows, our rages, our regrets up to the hungry moon until it is full before resting our well-worked feet atop the feet of our joys and letting them dance us around in the soft grass.

HEAVY

If it's too personal, he says, *you can tell me to shut up,*
but have you always been heavy?

I smile at his question the way I often do when someone tiptoes
around the word fat like its bones are made of damp packed sugar.
His avoidance, a reminder that once I also refused to say the word
for fear of making it too real, too permanent, an incantation of shame.
The man asking is in my water aerobics class at the YMCA.

Every Monday and Wednesday, we meet here to lunge and jump
and kick against the water, tantruming our bodies
against it in the name of exercise. He asks this question with eyes
fixed on a man two lanes over standing on the lip of the pool, a well-
oiled wind-up toy of muscle and sinew preparing to dive.
My workout partner tells me he used to have a body like that
and watches the swimmer like the arrival of a lover at long last
home from an interminable war
who walks past him and into the arms of another.

I know longing, but I don't know this particular longing.
I have been fat nearly my entire life, buoyant though not a strong
swimmer. I have longed for many people, none of them a previous
smaller version of myself. I have stared at smaller bodies wondering
what it might feel like to move through the world not so much like
a steamship through a hostile canal, but I always return
to my substantial and loyal body and the cargo of necessary it hauls.

MULTIMEDIA PORTRAIT OF THE ARTIST'S GRANDMA

the satisfying snap of the first fresh butter-
slick piece of movie theater popcorn giving in between the
set of your teeth / the delicate sound of the hosta leaves unrolling in
June / pockets reliably weighted with peppermints and crumpled
Kleenex / the absolute certainty that the metal garden shed smells like
gasoline and birdseed even right this moment / the highest setting on
the air conditioner dial because *you can put on more clothes than you
want me taking off right now* / wooden clothes pins holding wavy
potato chip bags closed / a life savings of rubber bands, plastic bags,
and that one box because it is a good box, everything wrapped in wax
paper, including the family photographs & last will and testament,
corners crisp in the basement chest freezer next to a package of
chicken thighs and those single-serving ice cream cups with little
wooden spoons you're not even sure they make anymore / the tiny
yellow sun on the sewing machine shining from the back bedroom
well into the night / the gold-edged pages of a Bible cracked open
before the sun's gold edge can crest in the sky, before even God stops
dreaming every morning / a daily bowl of Cheerios floating in the
perfect amount of milk, its own gospel of O's / the thunk of an
envelope fat with clipped coupons and newspaper articles
dropping onto the floor of my metal mailbox, the return address label
still holding a dead man's name like a traveling headstone / not the
down comforter itself but the warm air trapped between its feathers
/ every solitary tree in the middle of a field of corn or soybeans, the one
dutifully standing at the halfway point so the farmer might eat lunch
in the shade, resting against its base

THE WAY BACK: RECONSIDERED

I do still want her to curate an eruption of colorful blooms
through the hard littered earth,
a cloud of 90's R&B to sit thick in the air around her chevy Impala,
and I still want a good look at the decaying
remains of her cowardice laid out for burial.
I think though that she should be aware that her luck has run out
and, moreover, that she gave it the strong legs it left on.

I want her to wear my silence around her neck like an anchor,
a souvenir of the time I was willing to share even the most shadowed
corner of my kingdom with her, remind her how fortunate
she was to ever witness my softness, and how foolish
she was to misunderstand it as a weakness.

Now though, when the tithe is paid, I want her to go quietly away.

ONE DAY, MY EX'S NEW GIRLFRIEND WILL COME TO TAKE WHAT'S LEFT

I come across her standing on my front porch, opening my mail. She says she thought it was hers, swears she didn't even know I lived here, laughs off her "mistake," and fawns over my dress, pulls me into an embrace where she unzips and slides it from my body as we separate, shoving it into the hungry purse on her shoulder with my mail.

She welcomes herself in, stalks from room to room, painting the air with a cheap jasmine-oil-over-wet-fur musk. She doesn't think or doesn't care that I notice her hands on everything that has even the slightest sparkle or that she is slipping my mirrors from the wall into her bag next to my wilted dress. She leaves snarls of her long burgundy hair in place of everything she takes. She never looks me in the eye and I allow it all. I heard from somebody that things have started to go dull around her. She heard from someone else that I still shine. She has come here as an open-mouthed jar.

She is entirely bewildered when later that night, in her own home, she parades in front my mirrors and sees a jar of dead bugs in a dress that doesn't fit while I sit in my freshly looted apartment, smiling, naked, brilliant as ever.

QUESTIONNAIRE FOR FUTURE POTENTIAL PARTNERS

If you were a Beyoncé song, which one would you be?
Please explain your answer.
Do you now or have you ever worn a fedora unironically?
(If yes, please note the year and provide photos for burning.)
If I ask for an item in my purse, do you bring me the purse
or the item from my purse?
Will you be checking any baggage?
Will you be checking your ego?
Tell me about the last time you ugly cried.
On a scale of Joan Crawford to Clair Huxtable,
what is your relationship with your mother like?
Is there such a thing as too many pillows?
Are you an extrovert or a people pleaser?
Are you an introvert or a control freak?
Do you now or have you ever weaponized silence?
Describe a time you bucked the white supremacist patriarchy.
What font do you apologize in?
Do you love femmes or just femme labor?
What are you afraid of? How much does your fear run you?
Where does your worth live?
If I show you all the delicate parts of myself I have ransomed back
from the ungentle world, will you treat it like:
    a.   a weakness?
    b.   a commodity?
    c.   the most powerful part of me?

Be sure to show your work.

PEACHES

When I ask my therapist if it's me,
                 something about me
                 that people are always leaving?
she says, *Yes.*

She says, *You are the best and juiciest peach at the top of the tree.*
People's mouths water for you, but they are scared of your heights
and choose familiar peaches from the ground, even if they are rotting.
Do not throw yourself into the dirt for them.
They need to stop being lazy and climb.
It is you who keeps making them leave,
but it is you for all the best possible reasons.

SPELL FOR THE FULL MOON

Tonight the moon is a pulsing round button on a slot machine,
fat and ready to burst with light,
charged with now, now, now.
Let it be our lucky night; let it hit.
Let the stars fall with our payouts, our massive and much needed
wins, our jackpots gently carrying our heart-wants down to lay
in the dirt softened with our sobbing on desperate moonless nights.
Let us wake up when the moon has rolled back into its bed,
fully spent, to a bountiful harvest.

It is said
and so it is.

MISGUIDED LITTLE UNFORGIVABLE HIERARCHIES

Any muscle uncomfortably tensed for too long will still ache even
after it is at last relaxed. The sob that escapes my chest is a moth
that has been slamming itself against the glass for 30 years trying
to find a way out—not a hurt moth but a relief moth.

My therapist's walls are papered with moths.
Some of their wings look like eyes—
kind, maternal eyes—
some of them weep along with me,
all of them see me,
really see me,
witness me,
assure me that the trauma I carry into this office was not made up,
was not too small,
was not ever my fault.

BREAK UP WITH YOUR MOTHER, I'M SCARRED

After all of her lessons in what she called *strength* wherein she
would slink behind me and yank a vertebrate from my unsuspecting
spine then dare me not to collapse while she mocked my weaving
and dodged my hands reaching for motherly steadying. I honestly
believed she would be proud when I started learning to right
myself, first by pressing my back to the flowered walls when I
moved between rooms—
instead she called me closed off. I found friends and borrowed
mothers who happily assisted my balancing act—
she said I was codependent.
My little girl heart with its stitched lace edges spent a fortune in
waxy birthday wishes hoping to one day thrill my mother with my
ability to magic myself steadily upright after one of her severings.
Instead, I embarrassed her. She'd never
    meant for me
      to have anything better than she'd wanted.
  Her
  intention
    was never anything like
      strength.
    She'd seen my
  magic before
      I
      could and she
    feared it
      so much
 she meant to snuff
      it out
      the only way she knew how.
   Imagine,
   the unwitting
   gall I
   possessed
   to gift it to myself
   while looking her in the eye.

EXILIUM ANXIETATEM: A COUNTER CURSE FOR WITCHES WITH UNSETTLED SPIRITS RIDING THEIR SHOULDERS

When the backlog of blood ghosts grows too persistent
too aggressive in their attempts to collect on the debts you owe
focus
the lungs on their budding and blooming
slow
the heart back into time
smoke
the angry bees in your honeycomb head calm
coax
the lying stingers from under your skin
the venom doesn't dance through you
it never did
it was never true
it was never true
it was never true
everything here
is honey
sweet
slow
gold enough to pay the greedy specters off

FLOAT

Among the rules posted at the hotel pool is: *No swimming alone.*
The pool is completely deserted

save for the late 90s pop-rock tumbleweeds coming from unseen
speakers like someone left a window to the last decade ajar.
I   traveled here
                    alone.
So after a whole day of squeezing into airplane seats made for less
than half of my body,
the expanse of this heated, indoor, saltwater pool glittering
in front of me is a fortune I will not pass up.

My tightly wound spatial awareness drops with a clang at the edge
of the pool with an echo that only underlines the emptiness.
I slide into the water's arms without even a hint of strain.
I starfish on the surface of the pool.

There are people who cannot relax their bodies in water,
who sink or flail on contact.

How nice it would be to trust my body to love with the same ease
I trust it to the water,
to lie back in it,
let it hold me,

                    and float.

IN WHICH TWO WOMEN GO OVER A CLIFF AND RETELL TO LIVE ABOUT IT

For My Blud Sister Rachel M

In this retelling, the two women in the convertible are sisters in ache,
they are seasoning the pale Midwest
air with 90s hip-hop and ancestral cackles,
wearing giant hoop earrings and the gaudiest possible sunglasses,
hair whisked by the wind into cotton-candy beehives
nearly as feral as they. They have not murdered any men,
not literally, not yet, though they understand the need may arise.

They pull into drive-thrus for bucket-sized, ice-heavy Cokes
and towering twists of soft serve. They litter the shoulders
of the highway with bits of trauma they no longer wish to carry.
It lands at the feet of handsome drifter
archetype they won't be picking up –
he is as useless as his plot to woo and rob
the two women of everything
they've spent their lives saving.
His itchy hands could never hope to contain them.
The two women have no room for him anyway –
they travel with a backseat packed with dried roses and sage
and an entourage of ghosts so thick they have to ride
with the top down even in the rain.

In this retelling, the two women in the convertible will
not be cornered, will not be forced to choose
between a plummeting death
or man-handled justice.
In this retelling, the two women in the convertible
have already grasped one another's hands
and driven   off

                   the

                          cliff

astonishing everyone except themselves
when they make it to the other side.
They were always going to making it.

Everything ahead of them is

a victory lap.

PRAISE TO THE LONGEST NIGHT OF THE YEAR

Because the universe got jokes
my estranged mother steps out of her front door
at the exact moment I arrive
to deliver a birthday tradition
for my un-estranged stepdad's birthday
where I follow his late mother's holy recipe
and bring him a still warm pan of baked macaroni and cheese.

When my mother's eyes focus on the surprise of me
corporeal and doing just fine
her mouth is familiar
a scythe at the ready
but I am not afraid; not angry
I see how on the days I am short on mercy for myself
I almost look like her around the eyes.
I notice how much taller than her I am
despite her standing on the top step of the porch
to a house I still have keys to
but am not welcome inside of anymore.

Praise my therapist.
Praise the universe and its divine clownery.
Praise the chosen family who stay choosing me back.
Praise the mothering in me despite it not coming from her.

UNCONDITIONAL FIRES

Love,
no matter how grand,
is never a house,
though it could be a kitchen.

The kitchen is important,
though in the event the house were to burn,
leaving an exposed and miraculously intact kitchen,
it is not a place to live anymore.

If you are resourceful
and find use in the surviving love,
it does not have to corrode there in the burnt bones
of a once-was house.

There is so much that could be salvaged
and used piecemeal to revive kitchens otherwise in disrepair,
if you can bear to dismantle all the fire did not destroy,
or you could rebuild a new home around it
that is perhaps less vulnerable to fire.

ALL AT ONCE

*you are in love. / what does love look like?/...like everything i've ever / lost /
come back to me. – Nayyirah Waheed*

An abandoned city switches on with an electric gasp,
every fixture fitted with a gold-dipped light bulb.
The hum the light produces is as melodic as the glow is divine.
And
that hum, it revives the dried corpses of flower bouquets
hanging by their severed ankles. They resurrect
in a parade of technicolor, shucking the ribbons that bind their stems,
and as though this is not miracle enough,
they go in search of the roots they were ripped from—
more miraculous still, they are reunited,
reattached, and resume growing.
They grow and they grow and are still growing even right now.

The mascara-darkened tears of a shy fat girl
in the bathroom at the 7th grade Valentine's Day dance
come to an abrupt stop when she is bitten by an unshakable knowing
that a day will come that brings with it a pair of hands
that will love every inch of her still fat body sturdily and gently.

At the same time, with a long-held sigh, every rusted latch
on every rusted cage in a sedate and forgotten zoo
clangs open in unison. The beasts, the birds, the reptiles
paint a brand-new sky over top
the current one with their unfettered exultations.

The new stars in this new sky shine above a gray house
where a pair of hands exhumes a weathered cigar
box from under a loose floorboard, anticipating,
at best, a meager and hard-earned savings, instead finds that a fortune
has spread like a nesting virus beneath the house—the entire structure
sits atop a pulsing and eager windfall.

All the while a piano player wanders deep into an untamed landscape
where no one would think such a thing could survive
a magnificent church sits wearing vines like ropes of fine pearls
and inside, the most ornate organ like a heart.
No one has ever worshipped properly here.
The piano player comes inside, glides
her fingers tenderly across the keys. The way the sound
awakens under her fingers,
you would swear the hammers must be bouncing on uncovered spine.
The hymn these two make together writhe against the rafters
and pushes against the seams of the roof,
a praise song so warm it fogs the stained-glass windows,
a rolling, fearless hosanna that rattles even the gates of heaven.
There is no God who could claim not to hear it,
not a single deity who could resist
lifting their holy hands in benediction
to a love as destined as this one:
divine and miracle, humming and vibrant,
honest and abundant as ours,
a love capable of reviving even long dead things
and issuing pardons to their assassins.

ACKNOWLEDGEMENTS

Endless love and gratitude to;
 —Rachel McKibbens & Jacob Rakovan and alla them kids for being my family & my favorite place to runaway to.
 —Simone Person, for being THE homie and chasing shadows and throwing shade with me,
 —Ben Figueroa for staying on the phone and always walking me back from the edge or at least sitting down next to me on it,
 —Siaara Freeman for continuing to grow up with me,
 —Emily Gerson for basically everything.
 —Sean P Mette for still seeing and celebrating the wonder in the world,
 —Hope Hill, for being a regular reminder of what kindness and care look like,
 —My incredible therapist, Jennifer, for helping me organize my wild and unruly brain into something manageable.

Thank you to Jon Sands and all the wonderful Monday night folks from the Emotional Historians Workshops for reminding me of the joy waiting for us in writing.

As always, I am grateful to the wonderful team at Button Poetry; Sam Cook & Riley Lang for so often and so readily saying "yes" to me, my work, and even my frivolous requests.
Extra thanks to Tanesha Tyler for keeping all these plates spinning.

PREVIOUSLY PUBLISHED WORKS:

"Femme Fatale" was previously published in the 2019 edition of *Glass Poetry Journal*

"When the Fat Girl Stays Fat" was published in Volume 12 Issue 4 of *The Bitchin Kitsch*

ABOUT THE AUTHOR

Rachel Wiley is a queer, biracial poet and performer who aspires to one day move to the bottom of the ocean and become queen of the octopuses. While she waits, she is living in a cute little witch cottage in Cleveland, Ohio with her cat, Legendary Kitten Meowoncé Cathair, collecting stickers and vintage housewares.

She is a fellow and faculty member of the Pink Door Writing Retreat held annually for non-cis-het-male writers of color in upstate New York.

Rachel is the author *Fat Girl Finishing School* and *Nothing is Okay*, also published by Button Poetry.

OTHER BOOKS BY BUTTON POETRY

If you enjoyed this book, please consider checking out some of our others, below. Readers like you allow us to keep broadcasting and publishing. Thank you!

Neil Hilborn, *Our Numbered Days*
Hanif Abdurraqib, *The Crown Ain't Worth Much*
Sabrina Benaim, *Depression & Other Magic Tricks*
Rudy Francisco, *Helium*
Rachel Wiley, *Nothing Is Okay*
Neil Hilborn, *The Future*
Phil Kaye, *Date & Time*
Andrea Gibson, *Lord of the Butterflies*
Blythe Baird, *If My Body Could Speak*
Desireé Dallagiacomo, *SINK*
Dave Harris, *Patricide*
Michael Lee, *The Only Worlds We Know*
Raych Jackson, *Even the Saints Audition*
Brenna Twohy, *Swallowtail*
Porsha Olayiwola, *i shimmer sometimes, too*
Jared Singer, *Forgive Yourself These Tiny Acts of Self-Destruction*
Adam Falkner, *The Willies*
George Abraham, *Birthright*
Omar Holmon, *We Were All Someone Else Yesterday*
Rachel Wiley, *Fat Girl Finishing School*
Bianca Phipps, *crown noble*
Rudy Francisco, *I'll Fly Away*
Natasha T. Miller, *Butcher*
Kevin Kantor, *Please Come Off-Book*
Ollie Schminkey, *Dead Dad Jokes*
Reagan Myers, *Afterwards*
L.E. Bowman, *What I Learned From the Trees*
Patrick Roche, *A Socially Acceptable Breakdown*
Andrea Gibson, *You Better Be Lightning*

Available at buttonpoetry.com/shop and more!